Pilgrimage Through the Storm

by
BINDIYA B CHANRAI

Legal Publication Title Page

This edition first published 2024.
Copyright ©2024 Bindiya Chanrai. All rights reserved.

The right of the author Bindiya Chanrai to be identified as the author of this work has been asserted in accordance with law.

Author: Bindiya Chanrai, London UK
Literary Agent, Editor, Author Coach: Wendy Yorke; www.wendyyorke.com
Publisher: Parul Agrawal, www.serapisbeypublishing.com
Designer: Natasa Ivancevic

Limit of Liability/Disclaimer of Warranty

Paperback   (979-8-9907418-5-0)
ISBN

*This book is dedicated to all fellow travellers …
in our sharing lies our strength.*

Praise For This Book

"Today, I finished reading Bindiya's book for the second time. I can't wait to have my own copy to keep on my bedside table and to hold it close to my heart!

Reading Bindiya's words has been an immense privilege and from the opening lines I had this strong sense of 'this is what I have been longing for'. I didn't rush to finish it because I felt that to gulp it down would be a disservice both to the author and the transmission it offers. Often, I found myself reading a sentence, closing my eyes and meditating on what I had just read. As I read, I laughed, I cried, I breathed deeply and many times I said, Yes!

I read her manuscript while going through a dark time in my own life. Her words and prose brought me immediate relief. They were a much-needed balm and reading them I felt less alone and more understood. The cadence and style of her writing reminds me of those great poets such as: Mirabai; St Teresa of Avila; Gibran; Kabir; and Hafiz but, at the same time, she has her own inimitable style which I found to be unpretentious, honest and raw. With the rawness delivered with such grace that it soothes rather than jars.

As someone who helps people to sleep and who also sometimes struggles to let go of the day, I found reading her book to be so calming and safety inducing - even the parts that made me weep. I often read a page or two before turning out my bedside light, a closing prayer on particularly heartbreaking days.

While there is a part of me that wants to covetously hold on to her book like a 'best kept secret', I look forward to wholeheartedly recommending her beautiful work to everyone I know who is on this journey of consciousness and growth. It is not an easy journey and her book will undoubtedly serve as a solid companion along the way.

With my gratitude for the gift this book has given me."

Dr Nerina Ramlakhan, physiologist, sleep expert, speaker, and author of four published books, www.drnerina.com

"This exquisite book is in complete alignment with my spiritual path. The language used beautifully conveys the human struggle through poetry, and the frequency and tone is of a high vibration. It draws you in quickly and as the pages unfold you see yourself as you are right now. A person reading it with the intention to transform themselves can, and will, have an awakening experience … moreover, fuelling the impetus for self-enquiry.

Every soul on the planet is coming to their human self right now, seeking release from the old energetic patterns. Starting with the shadow self, this anthology serves as a beautiful reflection for anyone who wishes to explore their inner depths. Bindiya's creation is exceptional, and I will definitely recommend this first volume to my friends, family, colleagues and clients because I wholeheartedly believe its profound energy can truly benefit others."

Paul Quinton, founder and teacher of the Alignment Modalities, cranial sacral therapy, channeler for Spirit,

foundational psychotherapy, Reiki and Seichum Master and teacher, theta healing practitioner, sports massage therapist and Emmet techniques practitioner and author, www.alignmentmodality.com

"Bindiya's book takes you on a journey through uncertainty. She envelopes this experience with comfort from a divine source and presents it eloquently to the world. She meanders through nature, unravelling a modern understanding of what it may mean to be human. She gifts kindness, allurance and acceptance. Through avenues of fear, she throws love, creating a safe space for patience to fall through impatience in a dance between beings. There is no hierarchy in this unique exploration - only love - read this for yourself in complete awareness of who you are and see what unfolds."

Amy Grainger, The Time Keeper, modern-day philosopher and founder of the Souls of One's Feet, www.soulsofonesfeet.com

"The invisible architecture that held my life together

comes tumbling down, piece by piece.

I say nothing.

I do nothing.

I stand mute amongst the rubble.

I have entered the forest of the dark night."

Contents

CONTENTS

Introduction: The Womb

My eyes open with an unanticipated suddenness. I awaken with a fortress of pillows around me. Safe and secure in the silent darkness. There is a drop in my stomach, I remember. The self-created sanctuary of the womb a thing of the past. A dream shattered to pieces. The plug is out of the socket. I am switched off, absent from myself. Vanished, without a trace.

Did I ever exist? A deep detachment, an incongruence. A profound disharmony between the world inside me and the world around me. My skin is ripping at the seams, something inside me is desperate to get out. How will I lay this demon to rest? Feelings of fear grip my body and hold me hostage. Enveloped in a state of temporary paralysis; I am caged. The new day brings a promise of endless possibilities. I decide to return the gift unopened. Today's forecast; winds of despondency.

The womb beckons me – again – but it is time to face another day. There are things that need to be addressed. Things which have to be done, no matter what my circumstance. Sunrise, an order that must be obeyed. The mundane rituals bear the load of climbing a mountain. I wonder, is the thought of doing something more of a burden than actually doing it? And yet, these daily undertakings throw me a life ring; prevent me from drowning. These banal everyday responsibilities; the key to my sanity. The 'humanness' of my situation, both a blessing and a curse.

As I make a cup of tea, my eyes blankly rest on the world beyond the window. The barren trees and haunting, lonely skies are in commune with my reality. Autumn has come and gone with not so much as a whisper. The jewelled colours now faded leave me with a hollow heart. I am smothered in hues of grey, inhabiting this spartan landscape of gloom. Even the bitter chill that seeps into my bones does not wake me from this century old slumber. Yes, autumn has abandoned me with not so much as a goodbye. I have abandoned myself, with not so much as a goodbye. A subliminal sadness only magnified by the disappearance of the sun. Like a hamster in a cage, in a nomadic frenzy, I senselessly move from one thing to the next, leaving behind a trail of unfinished tasks. And then I pause, frozen, the all too familiar feeling of worry swoops in unannounced and bullies me into submission. A crippling vacuum shadows me all day. It seems the entire world is going about their business and I am forced to remain stationary. I stand with my open wound; reticent in its nature.

Yes, I exist, but in name only; I am not living. I switch on the television, hoping the images on the screen will somehow reconnect me. But to no avail. The sounds that filter through the radio have the same effect. I remain, quite simply, totally disconnected.

What gave me pleasure, is now reduced to nothing but a chore. What I looked forward to, now makes me want to hide in a box. However, I continue to put one foot in front of the other. I will get through today; as I did yesterday. Dawn will keep its promise tomorrow and arise as it always does. Perhaps, this is what my Beloved calls, unconditional love.

If I
(From My Beloved To Me)

If I gifted you the keys to the kingdom
Would you be prepared to open the door?

If I tore your house down and asked you to re-build,
Could you cement the foundations with self-love?

If I revealed all the answers lay within
Would you dare to take a peep inside?

If I said that without you, I remain incomplete,
Would you trust me? Take my word?

If I asked you to lift the veil, ever so slightly,
Would you be ready to meet the wonder that is you?

If I said your vulnerability is the most precious jewel of all,
Could you wear your wounds with eminence and pride?

If I shared that nothingness is the point from
which all joy emanates,
Could you possibly shift your perception?

If I dare you to dream to your heart's content,
Will you know that I will show up? Wave my wand?

If I could give you this day, whatever you wish,
What would you ask of me?

If I asked you to stop replaying the stories of your past,
Would you be willing to write a new script?

If I told you the adolescent needs care and nurture,
Would you consider taking her out to lunch?
Or, what if I said your inner child misses you,
Would you set up a playdate right away?

If I said that each and every of your moves
was etched in my reflection,
Would the thought of that make you fall in love with yourself?

If I promise you the universe, and so much more,
Will you Allow? Surrender? Accept?

If I, my Cherished One.
Will you?

Goodnight

Grant me the gift of a good night's sleep
Tame this monkey mind
Sprinkle my thoughts with fairy dust
Hush them as I rest

Come visit me Beloved, for I feel so alone
Entomb these shadows that haunt
Whisper sweet nothings, soothe me with your calm
Shelter me under your wing

Arrest my fears, condemn them to life
Slay the monsters that taunt me at night
Lay to rest what serves me no longer
So that I may dream once more

The colour of Oneness, the blackness of separation
Unmoored between the two
Be my lighthouse as I wrestle with the waves
Tenderly, guide me ashore

How I long for you to love me and be worthy of that love
Absorb me this night I pray
Is an answered prayer, a prayer that is heard?
In which case, where are you now?

Lost

The weight of the world on my shoulders
A cross too hard to bear.

Lost in a maze with no way out
Just me, myself, and I.

On my knees begging for mercy
My loud pleas lost in the wind.

Your formless nature brings unrest to my soul
Where do I go from here?

My Beloved Asks Me

Tell me what makes your heart truly sing,
What lights up your spirit with joy?

What is it that will ignite the bright, radiant spark,
Which lays dormant within your soul?

Where are you going, Dear One? This constant chasing ...
What is this non-existent completion you pursue?

Why constantly worry and dread the crossing?
When you have not yet reached the bridge?

Could you ride this wave and trust where it takes you?
Perhaps, be less humanly involved?

There is so much more than what meets your physical eyes.
Are you willing to take the plunge?
Step into that world?

Do you believe what lies before you is the truth absolute?
Or could it merely be the constructs of your mind?

You ask me to listen to your story and I am happy to oblige,
But is that the truth of who you really are?

Why not let it be, rather than let it go entirely?
Be more gentle, less hard on yourself?

Could you dissipate the loneliness by nurturing the longing?
Tend to each facet of your being with love?

"Shelter me under your wing," you say repeatedly.
Cherished One,
Where do you think you have been all this while?

Roommate

I live with a roommate.
We have been together for the longest time, as far back as this mind can recall.
She plays the roles of both companion and foe in my story.
She has more power over me than she knows.
My greatest advocate.
My optimum critic.
My ardent follower.
At times, when I crumple, she takes over and nurtures my crumpleness.
At other times, when I most need her, she abandons me.

I am sure you have guessed that roommate is I.

The only problem is,
We haven't actually met.

On The Cusp

Floating around the periphery of Beloved Union
Been here for the longest time.
Overbearingly tempted to succumb to you completely
But what would this mean in human terms?

Shed Light

Self-care, self-nurture, self-love
Forgiveness, release, surrender.
You throw these words around with no qualms
But refrain from giving any instruction.
No.
I am not as intelligent as you think, Beloved,
Please can you speak to me in ABC?

Genie In A Bottle

A home decorated with paperchains of enchantment,
Beautiful colours returning to my world.
To learn how to create from emptiness,
Spontaneous arrival of joy.

Perfect synchronicity,
Stars re-aligned, just for me.
To transcend the realm of make-believe
To be consciously connected to you.

A treasure trove of possibilities,
Profound union with the self.
To cross the threshold of authenticity,
Courage to voice my truth.

Release from festering worries,
Serenity, peace, calm.
To be a radiating vessel of love and benevolence,
To see only the goodness in man.

Resilience to endure the path of self-forgiveness,
For my history to longer dictate.
An amalgamation of all the selves,
For your will and my will to merge.

To recognise the clarity in paradox,
Your ability to discern.
Liberation from the false self,
And finally, (for now),
Restoration of my faith.

These are just a few of my wishes Beloved,
and if you like, you could tell me yours.

It was you who said I could ask for anything
Rest assured, I will be back to ask for more.

No Mercy

You silence my calls with your silence,
So be it
Mute, I shall remain.

You refuse to nestle in my heart,
A place
I had carved out especially for you.

You deem my worries insignificant,
And only add to my bucket of woes
I do not need you. I shall go elsewhere.

You bombard me with challenges insurmountable,
I walk barefoot
On the shards of glass.

You wound me into sadness,
Exacerbate my 'lossness'
Never will it possible to separate us two.

You push me off the mountain,
I am clutching at the clouds
In terror.

Oh Beloved,
Still, not a peep from you.

Astray

I have lost my bearings
I have stumbled onto the lion's tongue
His mouth is open, but only for now ...
I am on watch, but I am tired
Exhausted ... depleted ... done.
Eventually, I will let my guard down
And drift into slumber.
Beloved,
Will you promise to be there when he swallows me up?

Shame

They fall down and gain composure
I fall down and resign.

Beloved, perhaps it is time.

Time … I admit defeat

Time … to release all hold.

Human Nature

How quick they are to pass judgement.

Bang goes the hammer.

The sentence is passed.

The only problem is …

They never asked, Why?

Fear of Tomorrow

Lights off,
I am nowhere near ready,
The clocks are pressurising me
It is way past time for bed.

The ghouls of tomorrow are in their element,
It seems my Beloved is on sabbatical,
Which leaves me defenseless and unprotected.

Alone.

They think I will resist,
But I am voluntarily waiting to be slaughtered.

They can smell my fear,
Hiding is not an option.

They creep in on tiptoe
Why bother?
For I am, already, under their spell.

Black

Passing through the dark night, plunged into obscurity,
Deserted, remote, fragmented.
Caught up in the vortex, ruminating thoughts,
Consumed, with no room for escape.

Hanging by a string, wasting away,
The whims of this world my compass.
I beg, I beseech, radio silence,
My Beloved does not respond.

The gravity of my predicament, akin to a tsunami,
Destroying everything in its wake.
Swept in a tidal wave of intense isolation,
My identity enmeshed with my pain.

Self-sabotage in the form of shutdown,
The presence of absence my fate.
Self-constructed fears, which have no basis for existence,
Still,
They determine my path.

This tender heart breaks, time and time again,
Mourning the loss of dreams.
Hands tightly clasped together, I whimper in your shadow,
My Spirit crumbled to dust.

Behind these salty tears, loneliness rests,
How do I contain this grief?
Withdrawn and confined, a dungeon of my making.
Unseen. Unheard. Unknown.

Cracks in the mirror, estranged from my reflection,
Colours faded from my world.
Present in the physical, far removed from this reality,
You see me, but I am not really here.

This faith so brittle, it remains insecure,
This vulnerability so raw, it stings.
Paper thin hope frayed at the edges,
Beloved,
Rescue this wavering flame.

Unconditional Love

She planted bulbs with the best of intentions.
The sun gave unconditionally to her cause.

Lonely and bereft, she confided in the stars.
They guarded her secrets with their life.

She asked for grapes. Her Beloved gave her pears.
A crisis was avoided behind the scenes.

She awoke from a nightmare, finally ready to forgive.
A troop of angels had intervened as she slept.

Mystics prayed. She remained unaware.
Radical healings took place.

Her ancestors called a meeting and planned a surprise.
They cut the cords that tied her to a lineage of pain.

A stranger smiled.
With effort she reciprocated
Her heart was broken open.
Light moved in.

Every single new day was the birth of a miracle.
Her Beloved's eyes never left her side.

Fellow Travellers

Have you ever felt solitary in your pain?

Have you ever tried to join the dots and fallen off the page?

Have you ever housed an abundance of butterflies
in your stomach?
And not the happy kind?

Has loneliness ever visited, and engulfed you completely,
leaving you abandoned in the desert?

Have you woken at sunrise and yearned for the holding
silence of the night?
Or do a myriad of anxieties haunt you at sunset, leaving you
longing for the light of day?

Have you ever had blistering words resting on your tongue,
but a crippling inability to speak your truth?

Have you ever had a dialogue with your angels, only to be
followed by a crisis of faith?

Are you the storyteller who repeatedly terrorises yourself
with mindless fabrication?

Have you ever attached your identity to something outside of
you, and in turn lost yourself?

Or worn a mask for so long that you have forgotten where
the pretence ends and where you begin?

Are you so bound to your agony that you remain placidly still, as the world moves around you? Ahead of you?

Do you abide in several worlds, and yet belong to none?

Do you play several roles, but none of them define you?

Do you look for completion in all the wrong places, but fail to look within?

And you believe that you are solitary in your pain.

Walking In Fear

Walking in fear,
terror of the unknown.
It may happen,
but then again, it may not.
The potential of the present moment marred by the cruelty
of the unforeseen.
What a waste.
What an immense tragedy.
If only I could change my perspective.
No.
Choice is not an option.

The Choice Is Yours

Encased in a derelict chamber of darkness, I have been coerced here by my thoughts.

A tiny sliver of light peeps through a crack and tries to charm me, but I will not be seduced.

I remain on guard, suspicious, shrouded in my armour of resistance.

For I know the light is here only to illuminate my flaws, it has no intention of dispelling the darkness.

Instead of interacting with the light, I mingle with my hauntings.

Fear will be my muse.

Fellow travellers stand outside to say I am not alone …

Carrying lamps to light my path.

Go away. Get lost. Disappear.

I will not ease my burden by sharing; but instead morph into a shape that is so rigid, with no prospect of autonomy.

This is what I know best, so here I must stay.

Even the omnipresent One will not be allowed entry.

I remain at one with sentiments of seclusion and separation; putty in the hands of my futile thoughts.

The walls soak up my unhappiness and I am insulated in a porous case of gloom.

The darkness locked into each and every crevice of my experience.
Time will crawl slowly or perhaps not at all …
Lament tied to every tick of the clock.
This is how it has to be.
And so, it will remain.

***

Encased in a chamber of darkness, I have been coerced here by my thoughts.
A tiny sliver of light peeps through a crack, I stand back in awe and simply allow.
Exactly when I had lost all hope, the precious brilliance of infinite intelligence has found its way to me.
I want to interact and make the acquaintance of the light, but first I need to trust.
These cold surroundings bear no resemblance to the world I had envisaged but there is a way out.
Fellow travellers assemble outside, a gentle reminder that I am not alone.
They are here to cushion me, comfort me, carry me.
And I am profoundly grateful.
I salute the divinity that exists within them, realising that although our narratives may be dissimilar, we can absolutely gather and confer in our grief.
I gravitate towards the familiar for a moment, but conditioned responses serve no purpose anymore.
It has taken me a while to get here, but at last I am ready to usher in the light.
In this moment no sorrow, only the possibility of unlimited creation and expansion.

Perhaps in reality there is nothing to heal, only the truth to be revealed.
A snapshot into heaven.
And, so it will be.

****

The choice is yours.

Melancholy

You attached yourself to me, with no invitation
And there you set up your home.
My identity constructed by your imposing residence
You seeped into every part of my Soul.

Like harbouring a fugitive, I keep you secluded
The keys to the cell thrown away.
Forced into exile under your spell
I shrink, I droop, I withdraw.

Observing my surroundings, yearning to participate
You keep me a pariah among the rest.
Uninvited, nonetheless you rule with your cruelty
Devoured by the beast that is you.

Wellsprings of joy, tightly sealed by your nature
You break my Spirit, dismantle my worth.
You imbibe all that I loathe and despise,
Vulnerability, weakness, pain.

Forsaken in my loneliness, you reinforce my solitude
Oh, how I long to be cured of you.
Divorced from any conscience, you have no boundaries,
Enmeshed, intertwined, we remain.

The birth of a victim, the incarnation of a wall flower,
Your predative claws keep me bound.
I stagnate in the shadow of your oppressive closeness,
Two steps forward, ten steps back.

Haunted streets, empty hearts
Observing the world through your eyes.
You have inhabited me, wholly and completely.
Who is the prisoner?
You or I?

Joy

Doors wide open, a standing invitation.
When will you arrive? Come soon!
A host pacing impatiently in the dark.
She waits with her net ready to trap,
Enter a prisoner; for she will never let you go.

Beloved Counsel

To see your lack in the abundance of another
Trust me, Dear One,
This is a definitive gateway to hell.

To expect someone else to behave as you would,
in any given situation,
is contemptuous.
Nothing short of a crime against all parties involved.

To stew in a pot of stifling procrastination
And suffer in silence.
It is not a crime to ask for help.

To give to the point of emaciated, self-depletion
No good to anyone,
Least of all yourself.

To pull up the drawbridge and wither away muted.
Introversion is fine,
Avoidance will lead you to pain.

To live in terror of what may or may not be
This will only destroy you,
Tomorrow is simply a myth.

To say you are abandoned
Let me tell you a secret.

The point of abandonment can only be conceived
within the self.

To cast aspersions on the external
No joy to be found,
Turn within, turn within, turn within.

To say you will surrender
But only up to a point.
This is not surrender, you are only deluding yourself.

To plant the seed,
And then, doubt your faith ...

I promise you,
The rain is now on its way.

If I (From Me to My Beloved)

If I dedicate every breath to you
Will you promise to encompass my world?

If I open my heart to you completely
Will you paint my Universe with joy?

If I reveal my raw wounds and abort all censorship
Will you grace my Soul with your healing?

If I say your name when I am crumpled in a heap
Will you hold me tight in your arms?

If I affirm that, Yes, I am genuinely willing
Will you shadow me in all my endeavours?

If I place my complete trust in you
Will you promise not to make me look like a fool?

If I open the floodgates and cry my heart out
Will you pledge to acknowledge my pain?

If I were to speak my truth, what of the ripples?
Will you see me through the anger of the storm?

If I invite you to sit among the wreckage of my devastation
Will you help me to rebuild my life?

If I seek your reflection in the eyes of a stranger
Will you guard my faith in mankind?

If I take a few steps towards you, Dear One
Will you be there and meet me half way?

If I sit in solitude and await your guidance
Will you gently whisper into my ear?

If I stumble into the wilderness without a compass
Will you show up to guide me home?

If I, my Beloved
Will You?

Peace

To deepen into the stillness
When chaos threatens to reign.

To be gently seated in your feelings
Allow them to wash over your soul.

To be present to the nothingness
The infinite wisdom of no self.

To allow your past to guide you
As opposed to impeding your path.

To peel off the labels of judgement
Bow down to the unwanted guest.

To stop trying to escape yourself
Pay attention to the falling apart.

To kindle the flame of hope
When joy has lost all meaning for you.

To melt into the silence
In this quietude, the peace you seek.

To learn from the lessons of the soul
Hence, they always return.

To put your anxieties down on paper
Let the page hold the weight of your words.

To serve in each and every opportunity
Through which you know true bliss.

To lean into the enquiry
The answers unfold in time.

To be with the is-ness of all situations
In this being, your life transforms.

To shepherd the shadows with care
Light and dark are only one.

To gently coax your mind to take instruction from the heart
Every choice will be tempered with grace.

To caress every strand of your essence
True love must begin with you.

To be okay with losing your way, Dear One
And yes …
I will always show up and guide you home.

I Ask My Beloved

When will my purpose be realised, Beloved?
When will my vision breathe its first breath?

When will you pave the way before me,
So, I may dare to walk in your footsteps with pride?

I feel this world cannot accommodate me
Or is it 'I' who cannot accommodate this world?

You say everything is transient nothing is permanent
So then, what exactly is the point?

In our millions and billions, we pray to you,
Could you have overlooked me by any chance?

Beloved, do you make home visits?
In which case, could you put me next on the list?

You say there is nowhere to arrive at except where I am,
Then, do I have your permission to hole up and retreat?

Who is this 'I' I am trying to make happy,
When according to you the 'I' does not exist?

Badgering me for a surrender that appears irrational
and reckless,
How do I renounce my all to the one I cannot see?

You say I complete you, my Beloved,
But what exactly does this mean?

How can I, or will I, ever be able to inhabit authenticity
When I cannot articulate how I feel?

How can I stop resisting who I am
When it isn't an intentional choice?

If I make a conscious decision to compromise
what I say to another,
Will this make me an impostor in your eyes?

Consistently you refer to cause and effect,
Where does my soul contract fit into this mould?

You say that being overwhelmed by the darkness is not the
truth of who I really am,
But how do I separate the two?

I remain detached and removed on one level, yet somehow
functioning on another…
Something inside continues to move and breathe me,
my Beloved,
Could that be you?

Tough Love

You burden them like a donkey with baskets of expectations
Could you possibly carry some of the load?

Constantly embroiled in the drama of another
When it has absolutely nothing to do with you.

Crushed under a mound of unspoken words
You do not want to speak, nor will you let go.

How quickly you hand over your precious beads of joy
And blame others for robbing you of your bliss.

Self-imposed restrictions born out of pacifying others
Who is it who is holding you back?

Sharing your story but only to a certain point
They will have to decipher the rest on their own.

Always seeking validation outside of yourself
A folly, to say the least.

You give unconditionally, or so you say
Then, stand with your begging bowl waiting for
something in return.

Holding on with all your might, trying to control
Will you ever cut the ties that bind?

Consistently unthankful, breeding comparison
Nothing will ever be enough for you.

When you allowed the remarks of another to break your spirit
Did you not realise it was you who spoke?

They engage in idle whispers,
You listen … entertain.
Who is the one at fault?

Instead of remaining committed to a peaceful situation
You hold onto resentment and pain.

Creating a version of correct responses with
no room for expression
They will have to read the script exactly as you command.

You continue to project
They respond, as per your wishes
How unaware you remain of this power.

You dishonour yourself for the purpose of avoiding conflict
Who are you to call anyone a fraud?

Voluntarily, you conform in order to appease
And condemn the world for compromising your truth.

Caged by their perceptions, you say you are confined
Is it not you who has locked the door?

It is my highest intention to accompany you on this journey,
Dear One,
At the same time, I must be entirely honest with you.
Always by your side
I will shadow you eternally as you asked.
But first, would you like us to be friends?

Confession

I profess my conviction a million times.
But my actions tell another tale.

I say Yes, I trust and surrender.
But this is nothing short of a lie.

I share my desire to emulate your virtues.
But am an impostor who imitates and pretends.

I often preach to other people about you.
Yet, in each moment I question your existence.

I chant your name over and over again.
My entire being away elsewhere.

I like to think I am an embodiment of faith.
But do I truly believe?

I consistently ask you to handle my worries.
But this human mind takes centre stage.

I shamelessly measure your love for me
In accordance with the fulfilment of my wishes.

I ask for your protection 24/7.
But a huge part of me remains on guard.

I pretend that I am transitioning from selfish to selfless.
But am bound by earthly expectations.

I berate you for not responding to my call.
But where is the space for you to enter?

And yet … it is my relationship with you that remains
The most sacred of all in my life and hence
my need to confess.
It was never my intention to hurt your feelings, Beloved.
Only to tell you how I feel.

To be One with you; the purpose of this life.
And yes, I want us to be friends.

Fear Of Commitment

Before I commit, Beloved,
I need to trust that you know what you are doing.
For it is only this thought that keeps me sane.
Please forgive me, I need your reassurance.
As far as I am concerned,
Do you know what you are doing?

Labyrinth

Like a ghost in the desolate wilderness I tread,
Seeking escape from Maya*.
Confronted with one test after another,
The will to interact has died.

Challenging endeavours, distressing in their nature,
Prevent me from moving forward.
The threat of being swallowed up by these struggles,
Is robbing me of my peace.

Exposed to the elements, with no protection,
Unsafety suffuses my soul.
Betrayal of myself, immersed in separation,
What does it mean to be 'whole'?

Crushed remains, a haunting nothingness,
Impending blackness looms.
A dark empty space, my current residence,
Yearning to welcome the light.

Each decision I make, in a state of inertia,
It is the best that I can do.
A slave to the ebb and flow of my worries,
Not an ounce of trust in myself.

Memories deeply etched in my awareness,
Phantoms are living my life.
Ghosts from the past are holding me captive,
Every last droplet of power has run dry.

Hard lessons that must now be consciously imbibed,
A test of endurance I had not foreseen.
Will I be able to cremate my demons in this lifetime?
Or, will they follow me into the next?

Daunted by the prospect of a life unfulfilled,
But, where do I even begin?
Beyond my interpretation to assimilate,
Just how I got to this stage.

Round and round in circles I go,
Asking you Beloved, for a way out.
Your answer simple and yet it torments,
"The only way out is through."

(*Maya-Illusion)

Patience

Waiting for that day, Beloved,
When I can say to you with reprieve,
"Yes, it finally all makes sense."

The Visit

I was lacking and there, you arrived
The final piece of the puzzle in place.
The visit lasted a millisecond, if that.
But my life will never be the same again.
My heart smuggled right under my nose
And now, there is no turning back.

***

Being close to you, Beloved, makes me want to recluse.
It removes me from all that I know.
To be one with you intrinsic to my healing.
Yet, why does it instill me with fear?

You demand a profound unlearning,
a frightening resignation.
No promises, no immunity from pain.
My concrete reality smashed to smithereens.
No matter, I will not let go.

Give me permission to be solitary, Beloved,
So, I may savour your visit in peace.
In these pockets of silence, I will abdicate what remains
Until the 'I' exists no more.

An arduous path prickled with doubt and insecurity
Though to call it a sacrifice would be unjust.
How you came in all your glory and swept me off my feet.
And in the blink of an eye, you were gone.

What solace have you brought me? Are you aware
of my existence?
Left by the wayside to grieve,
A devotee rejected in the face of her devotion,
A desolate pilgrim, troubled and alone.

You are a paradigm of inconsistency, the only
constant in my life.
I am traumatised by the games you play.
Thinking that I was special, how wrong could I have been?
No different from all the rest.

The saboteurs are mocking me, saying I am deluded.
Nothing more but a sanguine dream.
Prove all of them wrong and preserve my dignity.
Beloved, will you please return to me?

In Gratitude

A deep yearning captured me to hide from myself,
You urged me to witness my reflection.

How I longed to dance aimlessly under the stars,
You entrusted me with a beautiful stillness.

I petitioned for my dreams to be realised in a heartbeat,
You granted me the virtue of patience.

And, when I wanted to escape into the world
of the superficial,
You entrusted me with deep introspection.

Time and again, disillusioned by humanity,
These teachers you offered for a purpose.

Dreams of building fanciful castles in the air,
You taught me to walk grounded on this earth.

On the brink of relinquishing this spiritual path …
Lovingly,
I was brought back to you.

Your ways remain a mystery.
You continue to astonish me.
Perhaps, I shall never understand you,
But my Beloved, I would have you no other way.

Prayer Of The Heart

Beloved,
With absolute reverence and belief, I soften into your grace.
I gently awaken to the realisation that all of life's tribulations
stem from separation, and I now choose to return home,
merged and eternally at One with you.

Yes, Beloved, with you as my support I need not ask for more.
I dispel whatever may be in my awareness that made me
falter from our union, knowing that infinite healing removes
all trace of what is unlike itself.
Knowing there is no power in precedence, I choose to
liberate myself from any engrained judgements, false beliefs
and limiting behaviours that may have blocked me from
fulfilling and appreciating my true potential.
I take a step back and watch in rapture as these are now
transformed into a new sense of Being.

I pour the burdens of my pain, ego and defences
into your lap
and as the spiritual warrior that I am,
I face the future with endurance, bravery and calm.
Those parts of me that I have denied expression,
I bring forth from the darkness into the light.
I profess my intention for healing and lovingly begin to
weave every strand of my being into the beautiful
tapestry that I am.
This is easy when I see myself as you see me.

As a point of Beloved Consciousness, all change begins with me and I affirm and confirm my intention to hold myself as sacred, and to cherish, love, respect, and care for myself.

I am finally willing to relinquish the identity that is preventing me from experiencing my highest good.

I look to the Spirit in each person that encompasses my world and choose to release any pain or sorrow that I may have endured.
I immerse myself in the divine practice of forgiveness, and start by forgiving myself for temporarily losing my way.
I free the people involved, and in turn I free myself.
Somewhere along the way, there was a meeting of our fears, but this is now dissolved into the nothingness from which it came forth.
Past hurts are now transmuted into exquisite treasures such as compassion, wisdom and enlightenment.

I do not have to create anything in this moment, only reveal the splendour and magnificence of my true nature, my authentic self.
As Spirit always supports its expression.

This is my heart's prayer and the divinity that burns bright within me shall illuminate my way and bless my each and every situation.

The entire universe dwells within the indivisible oneness of your love and, Beloved, I am nothing if not an extension of you.
And, so it is.

Divine Mystery

Elusive like a butterfly
Grounded in my consciousness.

Fickle like the wind
Anchored in my Soul.

Cryptic in your communication
A white feather comes my way.

The bearer of great suffering
A balm on these open wounds.

You drain me with your aloofness
And replenish me like no other.

Your silence disconcerts me
My most trusted confidante.

Exposed, vulnerable in your presence
The only place I feel protected.

Nowhere to be seen in this outer world
The master of my inner world.

Beguiled by the enigma I call my Beloved.

I Accept ... I Surrender

Rooted in the moment,
No past no future,
Cushioned in the awareness
This is for the best.
All is well.

Honouring my Soul contract
Aborting all questions,
Being present to this moment.

Unconscious choices welcomed
Dismantling of the ego,
I choose to get out of the way.

Resisting all labels
No 'Good' or 'Bad'
Accepting what unfolds.

Radiating your virtues
No matter my circumstance,
Breathing your truth everyday.

Trusting you blindly
With a rock solid faith,
Freefalling into your grace.

Turning left with nobleness
On my pre-destined path,
When all I wanted to do was turn right.

Each disappointment a catalyst
Each heartbreak a pilgrimage,
Nothing appeared in vain.

Today, for the first time
I pray with no expectations,
So, this is how it feels to be free.

I remain committed
To the promise I made,
You unlock the gateway to my Soul.

Staying on my chosen path,
Through torrential distractions,
Beloved,
My everything I gift to you.

Prayer

Divine Absolute.
All pervading consciousness.
No judgement.
No limitations.
Only is.

The gatekeeper who guards my fortress of secrets.
The chameleon who shapeshifts to accommodate my needs.
All powerful.
All present.
All knowing.

Your grace Beloved.
My knight in shining armour.
Your abundant blessings.
Raindrops in my desert,
I have never needed you more.

The One who has form in everything.
Content with no form of your own.
The One who moves the entire All.
Asking for nothing in return.
The One who responds to all who call.
With a humility so untainted, tender and pure.

Today, I pray to the One who I had temporarily forgotten.
Known to me as, my Beloved.

My Beloved.
You remain the one who eternally shadows me,
And I am he who lives, moves and has my being in your
shadow.
Enable me to consciously anchor myself in this truth.
So, it can manifest itself in every step I take.
In every thought I think.
In every word I speak.
In my each and every breath.

Recognising
There is only One,
I wrap myself around this pillar of divine union.
And I express with divine authority, my word for
self-expression.
I come to you with a skeletal spirit and hollow soul,
The beauty is, that you see me as whole.

As I share my thoughts with you, my Beloved,
Please be patient with me.
I am utterly confused and truly lost.
I ask that you allow me the privilege to simply be.
To express what needs to be expressed.
However inside out or upside down that may be.
To rest in your lap and unfurl.

My Beloved.
How and when my power slipped away from me,
I am not sure.
I only know that today I feel powerless and this is how it is.

I have lost my voice; displaced my sense of self; and am
completely adrift.
I live inside my head, amongst a plethora of stories and
distorted perceptions.

How can I possibly be the best version of myself in the face
of such adversity?
Although unaware, I find myself engaged in
self-limiting behaviours.
My mind is plagued by irrational fears and my vision clouded.
Could I be both the symptom and the cause?

I exist in a void.
A vast space of emptiness, intermittently pierced by a
sadness that stings.
Waiting in transition, hints of a promised land,
chasing a mirage.
My thoughts are broken and my devotion lacks sentiment.
Snippets of joy are floating around, too frightened to make
themselves known.
My sense of self is eroded, my responses conditioned.
And all choices stem from fear.
My entire consciousness is flooded with despair.

How can I escape myself?
Try as I might, it is a constant, consistent struggle to nest in
the present.
Shades of blankness cloak my existence.
A non-participation and enforced solitude that does not
seem out of choice.

My Beloved, can you receive my disconnection as a prayer?
Can you pray for me?

The suffering of separation,
Has infiltrated the entire landscape on which my
home is built.
The foundations are shaky and on the brink of collapse.
I have been sleepwalking.

I have inhabited a consciousness so far removed from the
truth of who I am,
That I can no longer discern what is real and what is not.

I am aware,
There is a power more permanent than the uncertainty of my
human thoughts.
At least, I know this with my logical mind,
But the knowing has not travelled to my heart … yet.

How can I step out of these self-created boundaries and
build a new life for myself?

I have been searching for a completeness in the outer world,
But to my dismay this does not exist.
I am desperate to befriend the stranger I have become,
And be in relationship with myself.

The level of transparency I share with you, my Beloved,
Is one no physical relationship can emulate.

Hence, I share my thoughts.

Speak to me, my Beloved.

Guide me in a way that this human mind can comprehend.

That is all I ask for now.

Tomorrow

To everything I say, "Tomorrow".
But Beloved,
Will that tomorrow ever come?

Let Go

Best laid plans,
A very human concept
Which has no place for the evolvement of my soul.
Deep-burning questions which serve no purpose.
All they do is induce pain.
What could have been …
What should have been …
What would have been …
The who …
The what …
The why …
Take it all, my Beloved.
Take it all.

Keys To The Kingdom

The road ahead of me is strewn with boulders and detours.
I stand at a fork with no direction.
Give without question, to the guidance you receive.

Where have you put me?
I do not belong.
Transcend the physical, but learn to live in its midst.

But I cannot make sense of what is happening around me.
Everything is going according to plan,
There are no shortcuts for the lessons of the soul.

Nothing is changing, my patience is worn to shreds.
That which is instant fades and is superficial.
What you acquire through endurance and time
is what remains.

What if anything can possibly be birthed from this space of
emptiness and desolation?
You may not believe it,
But in fact, the entire world.

How did my life get to be this way?
My rational mind is playing detective, trying to
locate a trigger.
Instruct it kindly albeit firmly, to abort the search.

What is the place of wishes in this life we lead?
Do dreams exist?
Always remember,
You cannot 'get'; you have to 'become'.

My selves have gone walkabout as the wandering gypsies
that they are.
If it is wholeness you desire,
With patience and loving acceptance harness them in.

My thoughts are akin to uninvited guests; intruding, trying to
break down the door.
Acknowledge them all through the peephole,
They need not be asked inside.

Distractions of every sort are trying to lure me into
their sticky web.
Like Buddha … do nothing, question nothing.
Be still and persevere.

How can I stay grounded in my being, in the light of
tumultuous external change?
When you find yourself at the heart of a tempest,
Remain the anchor,
Do not take on the shape of the storm.

Easier said than done.
Never forget you are a personification of pure Divine
consciousness.
Appearances are always changing.
Whatever the outward impression, the river will always
take you back to the sea.

The external world is my current reality,
but it continues to reimburse me
with what can only be described as an emptiness, a
hollowness.
**Nothing external can ever fill what you
are missing as a person.
Every desirable state that you wish to achieve
can only be permanently derived from the self.**

The things I thought are tangible are in fact a hallucination.
**This is a moment of pure potential.
Profound levels of awareness are beginning to emerge.**

But it is so difficult to separate myself from the content of
what is going on in my life.
This immersion is hampering my growth.
**Separation from Oneness arises from being merged with
the content of appearances.
Paradoxically, it is from that separation that you will
regain wholeness and unity.**

Sometimes I find myself stuck in a loop.
**What you are speaking of is your Soul contract; and its
purpose, is to return to conscious wholeness, the truth of
who you really are.
Lessons are repeated depending on how
you deal with them.
True liberation from these cycles hinges on how you
embody, assimilate and integrate them.
Although you may temporarily dodge these Soul growth
experiences, they will undoubtedly recur until you face
them and truly grasp what they are trying to teach you.**

So then, I shall eternally be at the mercy of life's challenges.
You are not a victim as you are where you are by choice.
Be it conditioned or conscious.

What is the difference?
Conditioned choices are patterns you were brought up
with, that over time have become the way in which you
interpret the world.
While a conscious choice is a soul level choice.

How do I navigate my negative feelings and
painful emotions,
without being devoured by them?
Do not compound your feelings through
judgement or labels.
Give yourself permission to own them, be with them,
make enquiries.
Approach with curiosity as opposed to condemnation.
Battling with your current mindset at any given time
brings immense suffering.
The more you fight something, Dear One, the more it
entrenches it.
Take a more gentle approach.

And what about surrender?
You think of surrender as having a kind of finality,
Let me advise, this is clearly not the case.
You are, and will continue to be provided with
opportunities for surrender.
Embrace it as a moment-by-moment process.

One day merges into the next ... time is ticking ...
what have I achieved?
**Smoke and mirrors,
The limitation of time exists only in your mind.
The present is eternity in absolute terms.**

Forgiveness is an empty concept,
One that I will never be able to discern.
**Think only about forgiving the self.
Do not concern yourself with anyone else.**

But it is so disheartening when we try our best
to practice kindness
and in turn individuals cause us pain.
**Another person can only hurt you when you relinquish
your power to them.
This is a voluntary act regardless of outer appearances.
When you think of an individual who has upset you,
ask yourself;
"What is it about being with this person that separates
me from myself?"
It is in your nature to practice love and compassion, and
I urge you not to tie your virtues to a sacrificial altar, but
remain true to who you are.
The more pain and suffering someone is in, the more they
inflict it on others, and this behaviour comes from their
own feeling of disempowerment.
Hand on heart, could you honestly say you would have
acted differently in any given situation?
It is not your job to make anyone better or different or
change them
in any way, shape or form.**

**Their behaviour stems from their own experience and
they are living out
their Soul contract in the same way as you.
These teachers have entered your life with intention and
are here to support you on your path to liberation.
Be grateful.
They are here to mentor, and provide you with the
lessons you yourself have chosen.
Nothing more, nothing less.**

I have been defeated, at least, this is how it feels.
There seems to be no escape of any sort.
**What you try to run away from will always get bigger
and when you try to silence the symptoms, they will
only get louder.
Stop running.
Give space for my messages to come through.**

I am treading an extremely fine line, Beloved,
and to go beyond it would mean unbearable exposure.
But if I were to turn back, I would only be betraying myself.
What shall I do?
Perhaps you have already answered the question.

But I am scared.
**Fear is nothing, if not a fallacy.
Walk directly into it.
Watch it evaporate and lose its hold.**

And what of sadness?
**If you had never met sadness, how can you possibly
recognise compassion?
Have you not noticed a new compassion in yourself that
has been cultivated as a result of your own sadness?**

**Go into your inner sanctum and ask yourself this:
"How can I turn my pain into a tool for greater change
and transformation?"**

That doesn't make pain any less painful.
**Pain is a useful signal that can indicate what is going on
inside you.
How else would you know what needs to be healed?**

I used to have an individual spiritual practice,
which provided me with beautiful inner peace and stillness.
It brought me back into alignment.
But now, this has lost all meaning for me.
**As you grow and deepen into your own, and the clarity
of your self-awareness increases, what worked for you
before will not come to the rescue anymore.
Such is the alchemy of transformation.
Be patient, metamorphosis never happened in a day.
All the doubt and uncertainty that you are presently
experiencing is in relation to the emergence of you and
the opening that is occurring within you.**

I could sit in a temple for days on end, or go on pilgrimage
after pilgrimage ...
Perhaps only then will you understand my
commitment to you.
**A place of worship albeit sacred, is not a magical carpet
that will transport you to the land of transformation.
It is only your belief that can precipitate this change.**

I feel as if I am not praying correctly,
or rather there is no emotion in my prayer.
How do I best talk to you?
**The potency of your prayer is in no way related
to fancy words
or any grand gestures for that matter.
Believe me when I say none of them impress me.
It is the volition in the words you speak that
melts my heart.
Sometimes, the most honest prayers come from that
space where we feel nothing.**

Rituals? Ceremony?
**It is indeed beautiful the way in which you light a candle
at the altar but, Dear One,
It is YOU that lights up the room.**

I am always expressing my gratitude to you but since we are
communicating so honestly, there is something I
need to share.
My gratitude comes from a space that can only be described
as disingenuous.
I do not exaggerate when I say that in every moment, I fear
That if I do not say thank you, you will snatch something
away from me.
**I am not here to take.
As I have said before, you are fulfilling your own
individual Soul contract.
So, please give this your consideration.
What you think of as trials, are merely inner
transformational experiences requested by you.
The purpose of these experiences is not to break you, but
quite the opposite.**

I want to be like you, Beloved.
But this is a losing battle.
Dear One, do you not know?
It is me who wants to emulate you and not the
other way around.

I am pleading with you,
What are the keys to the kingdom, my Beloved?
Banish all expectations to the land of no return
And most importantly,
Accept yourself, unequivocally, exactly where you are.

Journey Towards My Beloved

Entrenched in this battlefield of my own creation and held captive by human
perceptions, I finally begin the journey home, towards you, my Beloved.

Cemented in feelings of despair and having wandered like a nomad for what feels like an eternity, I courageously move one foot in front of the other, seeking respite from the storm.

With a broken heart and hopelessness encompassing my entire being, I take each step with a gentle determination, knowing that it is only in the shadow of your grace that the dawn of my healing shall arise and shine light on the truth.

With each step, this time of self-imposed exile is coming to an end.

Images of past hurts flash before my eyes, old wounds are triggered and that which needs healing is now being intensified.

Weary and exhausted, I approach your door and gently cross the threshold, knowing, that as I take this pivotal step, my life and identity as I know it, will never be the same again.

I stand before you, a living paradox, immersed in insecurity and hope.

With deep trust, I place my mask on the table knowing that in your reflection, my heartfelt supplication to be seen, will be granted.

All pretences discarded, I stand before you, vulnerable and exposed.

"Trust and surrender," you say to me and I am willing to comply.

My entire being I place in your hands, I am ready.
Ready to be unravelled, unwoven, undone.

The feeling of lead in my body slowly begins to dissipate as your unconditional love permeates and softens my each and every cell.

I lay down the backpack that carries the heavy burden of my history, knowing that I no longer wish to hold onto the past.

I look to you and say, "I have shown up, it is all that I can do."

The look of love in your eyes tells me that this is enough.
Lovingly, you embrace me and I feel safe and held in your tender protection.

Gently you whisper in my ear, "Come, my Cherished One. Let us begin our work."

Trust me.

Give in to this invitation.

Your Beloved has been pining for you.

Captive tears, allow the dam to burst.

Muted rage, scream as loud as you like.

Whatever troubles you, I am ready to receive.

Notes

Notes

Notes

Notes

Printed in Great Britain
by Amazon

55915680R00048